5 4 3 2 1   17 16 15 14 13

ISBN 978-3-88117-905-8

Translation: Nadja Rosental
Editing: Freya Gehrke
Layout: FSM Premedia

Printed in China

www.hoelker-verlag.de

Rose Marie Schulze

The Little
Berlin
Cookbook

Hölker Verlag

Contents

»Ene jut jebratene Jans
is ene jute Jabe Jottes«

Berlin, I love you, I could eat you up

When I think about Berlin and its cuisine, a thousand things spring to mind: the Kurfürstendamm avenue and Café Kranzler, Heinrich Zille and my favourite corner pub, the proverbial Berlin air and knuckle of pork, the KaDeWe department store and Kennedy's now legendary "Ich bin ein Berliner"(I am a Berliner) speech.

But what exactly is a Berliner, in a city where the individual districts – such as Steglitz, Charlottenburg, Mitte and Pankow – have as many residents as a normal big city? The city is truly enormous: from north to south it spans 50 kilometres, and from west to east it's even bigger. The people of Berlin live in their own *Kiez*, as the locals say, their own district. And they don't much like leaving it. Because everything you need is nearby. And why should someone from Grunewald ever visit Kreuzberg, or someone from Friedrichshain go to Lichterfelde? It's true, our capital Berlin is a city of the world, but Berliners themselves are loyal Kreuzbergers, Neuköllners or Lichtenraders. They live their lives in their own neighbourhoods: in the corner pub, having a chat and a gossip in the baker's shop, by the *Currywurst* or döner kebab stand. The original Berliner is now a rarity, but the new Berliners take the city's art, culture and cuisine almost as seriously.

The culinary landscape of Berlin is a potpourri of imports – over the course of the city's 700-year history, immigrants from Mecklenburg, Pomerania, East Prussia, Silesia and France have left their culinary marks. And that's what makes Berlin so cosmopolitan, inquisitive and integrating. When it comes to the city's cuisine, assimilation often went hand in hand with simplification with little room for elaborate preparation methods or intricate seasonings. Most dishes are simple and down-to-earth, wholesome and filling.

In the 17th century, Calvinist Huguenots came to Berlin from France and brought with them ingredients such as asparagus, peas, beans, cauliflower, cucumbers and lettuce. Soon all this was cultivated on the sandy soils in the areas around the city, complementing the rather stark diet of the Berliners, which had previously been dominated by cabbage and turnips. They also left behind a real weakness for *Frikadellen* – a type of meatball the Berliners lovingly refer to as *Buletten*.

Frederick the Great, the "French Frederick", with his slogan, "Let every man seek heaven in his own fashion", urged the Berliners to take a liberal and cosmopolitan attitude. And he taught them to eat potatoes in the 18th century, and inflicted on them high salt consumption. Ever since, potatoes boiled in their skins and served with quark and linseed oil, or peeled boiled potatoes with various dips, sour or salted preserved cucumbers and herring have formed an integral part of Berlin's cuisine.

Berlin's bars and pubs don't have set closing times, and so you can *rinschaufeln* as they say in Berlin (shovel down, stuff yourself), around the clock. Typical dishes include the *Broiler* (rotisserie chicken) and cold meat in a bread roll (*Schrippe*), and rollmops. Fried and marinated herring and pickled gherkins are a must and you will find *Buletten* everywhere.

These are some of the characteristic dishes from Berlin, whether you're eating out or eating at home: *Eisbein* (cured knuckle of pork) with sauerkraut and mashed peas, *Stolzer Heinrich* ("Proud Henry" – bratwurst with beer sauce), fried liver with apple and onion and mashed potatoes, chicken fricassee, Königsberg meatballs in a white caper sauce, or roast goose with red or green cabbage and potato dumplings. Fish dishes such as pike-perch with stewed cucumber, and eel or "green pike" are integral to the cuisine of Berlin. *Futtern wie bei Muttern* ("eat like you do at your mother's" – i.e. home-style cooking) is ultimately a question of quantity. And if you eat in one of Berlin's traditional restaurants or pubs, whatever is left over is wrapped in tin foil for you to take home as a matter of course.

These dishes are served with *Molle* (beer), *Kristallweizen* (NB: not the unfiltered variety of wheat beer) or the famous *Weiße mit Schuss* – a top-fermented, light beer that is brewed only in Berlin and is typically served with raspberry or sweet woodruff syrup in a hemispherical glass. Then you wash down a piece of crumble cake or pastry with *Muckefuck* (chicory coffee) or a new-fangled latte, after which you typically enjoy a little liqueur.

Berlin is certainly worth a visit – because of the *Berliner Luft* (Berlin air), if nothing else, which smells of the typical *Milljöh* (milieu) and of freedom. And the city's traditional restaurants and pubs are a very special experience indeed, where you'll really get to know Berlin's original cuisine. I hope all this will inspire you to try out the hearty and delicious recipes in this book yourself, to spoil yourself and your loved ones.

Guten Appetit and happy cooking!
Yours, Rose Marie Schulze

Snacks – from meatballs to curried sausage

Open sandwiches & more

Over the course of their history, the Berliners have starved more than once, which is probably one of the reasons for their great love of bread and butter, the Butterstulle. They even have an annual feast day in its honour. The slice of bread was eaten im Janzen, as a whole piece. Only gradually did the so-called *Beamten-Schiebewurst* become more popular: a buttered slice of bread with a single piece of cold meat on top, which was moved back a bit with each bite so that you had some meat left over until the end. These days the open sandwich always has plenty of topping, and today's Berliners love the *Klappstulle*: made, for example, with slices of egg, ham, cheese and/or cold meat between two slices of buttered bread – a Berlin sandwich.

"Schusterjungen" bread roll with goose fat

Schusterjungen are irregularly shaped bread rolls, traditionally made from rye and wheat flour. They are generally served as a hearty pub snack with goose fat and pork dripping, Hackepeter (spiced pork mince, recipe p. 13) or Harz (hand-moulded sour milk) cheese. Simple *Schmalzstullen* – rye bread thickly spread with pork dripping – are also very popular with Berliners.

750 g fresh goose fat, 2 onions,
2 fairly sour apples (such as russet),
2 stems of chopped mugwort, salt,
4–8 fresh *Schusterjungen*

Chop the fat into the smallest possible pieces and simmer until clear over medium heat in a wide saucepan containing 100 millilitres of water. Peel and mince the onions. Peel, quarter, core, and dice the apples. Fry the onion in the fat to a golden brown. Remove from the heat, stir in the chopped apple and wormwood, season with salt and pour the fat into a suitable container (traditionally an earthenware dish). Leave to cool and solidify. To serve, cut the *Schusterjungen* in half and spread thickly with fat.

Cured salted eggs

These salted eggs come from the town of Halle, which used to be a centre of the salt trade. The workers put the eggs in nets and submerged them in boiling brine to supplement their meals. In Berlin the salted eggs were popularised in the pubs. The eggs, which were boiled in their shells and placed in a concentrated salt and spice solution, used to be (and often still are) kept in tall glass jars, or Hungertürme (hunger towers), at the bar. If you felt like a snack, you could order 1, 2 or 3 eggs. They were then peeled, halved, spread thickly with mustard, and seasoned with salt and pepper before being served.

150 g salt, 2 bay leaves, 10 allspice berries,
10 peppercorns, 3 juniper berries,
15 dried dill blossoms, 1 onion, 10 large eggs

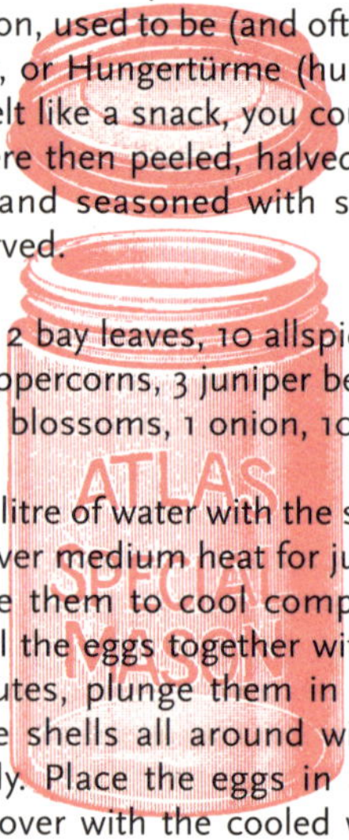

Bring to a boil 1 litre of water with the spices and allow them to steep over medium heat for just under 5 minutes, then leave them to cool completely. Peel the onion. Hard-boil the eggs together with the onion for around 10 minutes, plunge them in cold water and gently crack the shells all around without breaking them completely. Place the eggs in a tall container (with lid) and cover with the cooled water they were boiled in. Allow to steep for at least 24 hours (or even better for 1 week) in a cool place. To serve, shell and season as required.

"Strammer Max"

4 thick slices of rye bread, 2 tbsp butter,
200 g raw cured minced ham, 1 tbsp cooking oil,
8 eggs, salt, freshly ground pepper, 1 tbsp freshly
chopped parsley, 8 tomato quarters, 1 gherkin, sliced

Spread each slice of bread with some butter and sprinkle with diced ham. Heat the remaining butter and oil in a pan and fry the eggs in it. Place two on each slice of bread. Season with salt and pepper, and garnish with parsley, tomato quarters and slices of gherkin.

"Hackepeter" (minced raw pork)

500 g well-marbled pork (neck or leg), 3 onions,
salt, freshly ground pepper, fresh bread rolls

Use a meat grinder with a coarse blade to mince the meat. Peel and mince the onions. Put aside two thirds to use as garnish later. Mix the rest with the minced pork, season generously with salt and pepper, and garnish with the diced onion. Enjoy immediately on bread rolls. Turn the rest into meatballs (recipe p. 14).

In Berlin you can buy Hackepeter freshly prepared at the butcher shop or in supermarkets.

"Buletten" (meatballs)

Meatballs, or *Buletten,* are among the Berliners' favourite dishes. They are eaten hot or cold, with pickled gherkins, with mustard or without, on their own or on a bread roll – it doesn't matter, or it's *ejal* as they say in Berlin, as long as they taste like mother made them. They are eaten in the local pub, as a take-away snack or at home. And at home they're served with sauerkraut and called *Pferdeäppel auf Heu* ("horse apples" – dung – on hay) – this goes with fried potatoes of course...

The word *Bulette* comes from the French for little ball, *boulette*, because these meatballs were handed down to the Berliners by the French Huguenots. The following recipe follows the original and uses only pork, but these days a mince made of equal quantities of pork and beef is more common.

2 bread rolls, 1 large onion, 500 g minced pork, 1 egg, salt, freshly ground pepper, 5 tbsp cooking oil, 1 tbsp butter

Cut the bread rolls into thin slices, put them in a bowl, cover with lukewarm water and leave to soak. In the meantime, peel and mince the onion. Knead the mince, egg and well-squeezed slices of bread into a homogenous dough. Season with salt and pepper.

With damp hands, shape the mixture into around 8 even-sized balls and press down lightly. Heat the vegetable oil in a large pan and sear the meatballs on both sides. Reduce heat and finish frying them at medium heat for just under 10 minutes while also adding the butter. Drain on kitchen roll and serve.

The more you press out the bread rolls, the firmer the consistency of the meatballs. How soft they should be is a matter of opinion. As the Berliners would say: "jedem das Seine", to each their own!

Potato salad with bockwurst sausage

The famous bockwurst – a boiled sausage in a natural sausage casing, usually smoked – was invented in 1889 by Richard Scholtz, a restaurant owner from Berlin. He served it in his restaurant together with bock beer, and so his guests called it a bock-wurst. And you simply have to eat it in the traditional way, with a local potato salad accompanied by bread rolls and mustard!

1 kg freshly boiled unpeeled waxy potatoes,
4 hardboiled eggs, 1 onion, 200 g gherkins,
2 very fresh egg yolks, 1 tbsp hot mustard,
100 ml vegetable oil, 2 tbsp white wine vinegar, salt,
freshly ground pepper, 2 tbsp chopped parsley,
4 hot bockwurst sausages, 4 bread rolls,
hot or sweet mustard

Allow the potatoes to cool for a moment and peel them, slice them and place them in a bowl. Peel the eggs and, using an egg slicer, slice them once lengthwise and once crosswise into small cubes. Peel the onions and mince them and the gherkins. Add everything to the potatoes. With an electric mixer, mix the egg yolk and the mustard. Gradually add the oil to make a creamy mayonnaise. Season with vinegar, salt and pepper, and carefully mix it with the ingredients in the bowl. Cover with cling film and leave for 1–2 hours. Before serving, season the salad to taste and sprinkle it with parsley. Put the potato salad onto plates and place 1 bockwurst on top. Serve with bread rolls and mustard.

I have an old Berliner potato salad recipe in my collection that consists of nothing but potatoes, oil, vinegar, diced onion, salt and pepper. But potato salad with mayonnaise has now become the norm in Berlin.

Curried sausage and chips

Herta Heuwer, the former owner of a snack stand at the corner of Kantstraße/Kaiser-Friedrich-Straße, has given the Berliners a very special gift: she invented the *Currywurst*, the curried sausage. For the first time on 4 September 1949 she served a fried sausage with a sauce made from tomato puree, curry powder, Worcestershire sauce and a few secret ingredients. Today there is a plaque commemorating Ms Heuwer on that very spot. There is no doubt that, over the course of its ascent in popularity, the *Currywurst* has replaced the *Bockwurst* as the Berliners' favourite.

If you want to do it properly, you eat a curried sausage at the snack stand, the *Bude*, or in your local pub along with your chums. It's served with a *Molle* (beer) and plenty of napkins, because it will get messy. And then there is always the eternal question: "With or without casing?" – because when it comes to sausage casing, Berliners don't agree. Here is my suggestion for how to make curried sausage at home.

1 kg waxy potatoes, 1 kg deep frying fat,
4 bratwurst sausages, tomato ketchup,
Worcestershire sauce and curry powder to taste

Peel the potatoes. Using a potato cutter, cut out the chips and dry them with kitchen towel.

Heat the deep frying fat to 140–180 °C in a pan or deep fryer and fry the chips in batches to a light yellow colour. Remove and drain on kitchen towel.

Heat the charcoal grill and grill the bratwurst sausages on it (or fry them in a grill pan). Remove, slice and keep warm. Season the ketchup with Worcestershire sauce.

Heat the fat to 190 °C and deep fry the chips a second time until golden brown. Remove, briefly drain on kitchen towel and put on plates. Place the sausage slices next to them, cover with the spiced ketchup and dust with curry powder. Serve immediately.

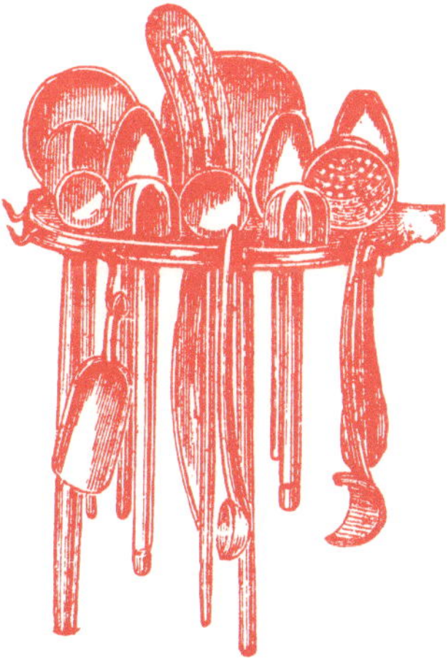

Berlin-style Döner kebab from Kreuzberg

At the end of the 60s, kebab shop owner Kadir Nurman from Kreuzberg found a way of making the Turkish dish, traditionally served on a plate, attractive to the Berliners: in the döner kebab pocket, the *Dönertasche*. These days, Berlin has more döner kebab shops per capita than Istanbul and the döner is as much part of the snack culture as the curried sausage. Berliners would never dream of making a döner kebab at home, even though it's really quite easy. This is a recipe for all non-Berliners who don't have a first-class döner kebab shop just around the corner.

600 g lean veal, salt, freshly ground pepper, 1/2 tbsp Döner kebab spice (or pul biber), kebab skewers, 2 onions, 5 tbsp olive oil, 150 g sheep's milk yoghurt, 2 garlic cloves, 1 tbsp freshly chopped parsley, 4 small flat breads (pita), 2 flavoursome tomatoes, 150 g red cabbage, 150 g cucumber

Preheat the charcoal grill or the oven to 220 °C. Slice the veal thin and season it with salt, pepper and Döner kebab spice. Thread it onto 4 skewers. Peel the onions and grate one of them on the fine side of a kitchen grater. Mix the grated onion with half the oil and brush the meat slices with it. Place the skewers on a rack and grill them for about 20 minutes on the charcoal grill or in the middle of the oven, turning them occasionally.

In the meantime, mix the yoghurt in a bowl. Peel and crush the garlic and mix it into the yoghurt. Season the yoghurt with parsley, salt and pepper.

Cut open the flatbreads and sprinkle the insides with the remaining olive oil. Remove stems from tomatoes and dice. Wash the red cabbage and cut into very thin strips. Wash the cucumber and coarsely grate with a kitchen grater. Halve the second onion and cut into wafer-thin slices.

5–8 minutes before the kebabs are done, put the flat breads on the grill or the bottom of the oven to warm. Remove the skewers and bread. Remove the pieces of meat from the skewers and put into the flat breads; add the other prepared ingredients to taste and slather with the yoghurt sauce.

Bismarck herring

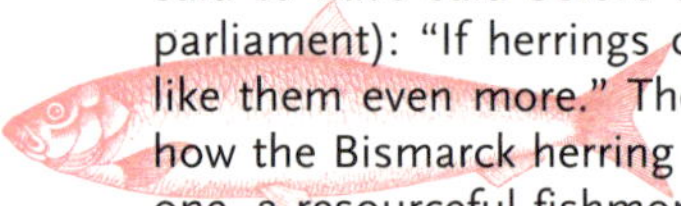

Imperial Chancellor Otto von Bismarck (1815–1898) is said to have said before the Reichstag (the imperial parliament): "If herrings cost a thaler, people would like them even more." There are many stories about how the Bismarck herring got its name. According to one, a resourceful fishmonger from Stralsund named Friedrich Wiechmann gave Bismarck a little keg of boned and pickled Baltic herring for his birthday. By way of thanks, Bismarck gave him the permission to sell this type of marinated herring under the name of Bismarck herring.

12 fresh herrings (prepared by the fishmonger), 4 tbsp salt, 1/2 l dry white wine, 1/4 l white wine vinegar, 1 tbsp sugar, 2 large onions, 2 carrots, 5 bay leaves, 2 tbsp peppercorns, 2 tbsp allspice berries

Rinse the herrings under cold running water and pat them dry with kitchen towel. Rub them with salt, cover them with cling film and leave them to marinate in the fridge for at least 2 hours.

In the meantime, boil 1/2 litre of water with the wine, vinegar and sugar. Remove from the heat and allow to cool completely. Peel the onions and slice them into rings. Peel and slice the carrots. Rinse the herrings and pat them dry. Layer them with the onion rings, carrot slices, bay leaves, pepper and allspice berries in an earthenware pot. Fully cover with the cooled down stock. Seal the pot with foil and allow the herring to infuse for 48–60 hours in a cool place. Before serving, remove the pickled herrings from the pot, wipe off the spices and put on plates. Serve with potatoes boiled in their skins, fresh onion rings and gherkins.

"Heringsstippe" (herring in sauce)

12 Bismarck herrings (recipe p. 22), 2 sour apples (such as russet), 2 onions, 2 gherkins, 150 g mayonnaise, 150 g sour cream, 4–5 tbsp milk, 1 pinch sugar, salt, freshly ground pepper

Remove the marinated Bismarck herrings from the liquid, rinse them, pat them dry with kitchen towel and cut them into lengthwise strips. Halve, core, and dice the apples leaving the skins on. Peel the onions and mince them and the gherkins.

Mix together the mayonnaise and the sour cream until creamy and season with sugar, salt and pepper. Carefully fold in the prepared ingredients and again season to taste. Serve with wholemeal bread and butter or potatoes boiled in their skins.

Rollmops herring

To make rollmops, a very typical Berlin dish, you use gutted and salt-pickled herrings.

12 salted herrings (or matjes filets), 1 tbsp hot mustard, 1 onion, 2 gherkins, 1 tbsp pickled capers, 1 tbsp peppercorns, a few cocktail sticks, 1/4 l white wine vinegar, 2 bay leaves, 1 pinch sugar

Rinse the salted herrings under cold running water and pat dry with kitchen towel. Place them side by side on the kitchen worktop and slather them with a little mustard. Peel the onion, and cut into fine strips, slice the gherkins, and layer both on top of the filets. Sprinkle with the capers and pepper. Roll them up and secure them with cocktail sticks.

Bring to a boil 1/2 litre of water with vinegar, bay leaves and sugar; then remove from the heat and let cool. Layer the rollmops in an earthenware dish and cover with the cold liquid. Cover the dish with foil and leave to stand for at least 24 hours.

These taste great with butterd bread or *Schusterjungen*.

Rollmops are a typical pub snack – and an excellent hangover cure after a night of partying.

Pickled fried herring

1 kg fresh herrings, juice of 1 lemon, salt,
freshly ground pepper, 3 tbsp flour,
2 tbsp vegetable oil, 50 g clarified butter,
1/4 l white wine vinegar, 1/4 tbsp peppercorns,
1/4 tsp coriander seeds, 1 tbsp mustard seeds,
2 bay leaves, 2 large onions, 1 salted gherkin

Rinse the herrings under cold running water and pat dry with kitchen towel. Sprinkle with lemon juice, season with salt and pepper, and coat in flour.

Heat the oil and clarified butter in a large pan and fry the herrings for about 10 minutes or until brown and crisp on all sides. Remove from the pan and leave to cool on kitchen towel.

Bring to a boil 1/4 litre of water with vinegar, peppercorns, coriander seeds, mustard seeds and bay leaves, remove from heat and leave to cool.

Peel and slice the onions. Slice the gherkin. Layer the cold herrings and the onion and gherkin slices in an earthenware dish. Pour the cold bouillon over them, cover and leave to marinate for at least 24 hours.

Take the fried herrings out of the marinade and serve with fried potatoes and salted gherkins (NB: not the kind pickled in vinegar).

Soups and stews – not just with lentils and peas

Beer soup with bacon

1 large onion, 2 bread rolls, 2 tbsp butter,
400 ml stock, 400 ml Berliner Weiße beer,
100 ml cream, salt, freshly ground pepper, 75 g diced cured bacon, 2 tbsp chopped chives

Peel the onions, and mince. Dice the bread rolls to 1 cm cubes. Heat the butter in a pan, sauté the diced onions for a few minutes, add the diced bread rolls and sauté to a golden brown. Deglaze with the stock, beer and cream and simmer the soup for about 15 minutes. In the meantime, fry the bacon over medium heat. Season the soup with salt and pepper, ladle it into 4 heated soup bowls and sprinkle some bacon in the centre of each bowl. Sprinkle with the chopped chives and serve.

For extra pungency stir in 100 grams of grated Emmental just before serving.

Potato soup "Emperor Wilhelm II"

Potato soup is said to have been the favourite dish of Emperor Wilhelm II – hence the name.

1 small onion, 100 g boiled ham, 100 g celeriac, 1 carrot, 2 Teltow turnips, 800 g potatoes, 1 tbsp vegetable oil, 1 tbsp butter, salt, freshly ground pepper, 1 generous pinch freshly grated nutmeg, 1 bay leaf, 1 l chicken stock, 100 ml cream, 1 egg, 8 stems parsley, minced

Peel the onion, and mince it and the ham. Clean and/or peel the celeriac, carrot and turnips and cut into small pieces. Peel the potatoes and cut into even-sized pieces.

Heat the oil and butter in a pan and sauté the minced onion and ham. Gradually add the rest of the vegetables. Season with salt, pepper and nutmeg. Add the bay leaves and pour the chicken stock into the pan. Bring to a boil, reduce the heat and leave to simmer for 25 minutes. Remove from the heat, stir in the cream and puree the soup with a hand blender. Pour one ladle of soup into a bowl, whisk the egg into it and stir it back into the soup. Season to taste, sprinkle with the parsley and serve immediately.

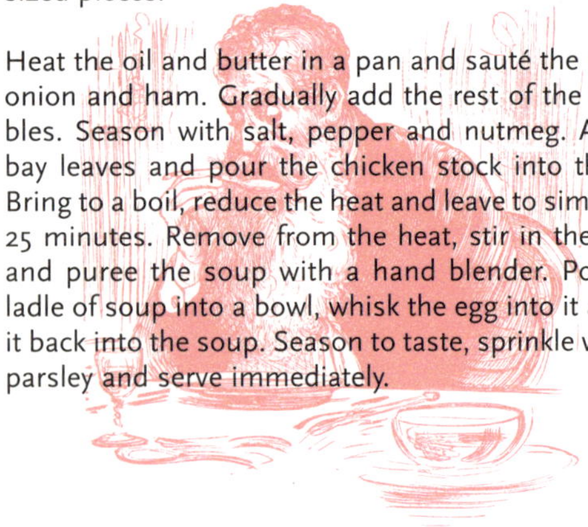

Swede stew

When times were tough – and there have been many of those times in Berlin – people didn't eat a roast on a Sunday, they ate a thin stew. Swedes, a hardy and affordable vegetable, used to be synonymous with sating hunger when times were hard. These days, Berliners sup their swede stew with great pleasure again – but enriched with a good helping of bacon.

1 small onion, 150 g smoked streaky bacon,
1 swede weighing around 800 g, small mirepoix of carrot and parsley root or celeriac with leek and parsley (or similar), 2 tbsp vegetable oil, salt, freshly ground pepper, 1 l meat stock,
150 g sour cream, 1 bunch parsley, minced

Peel the onion, and mince it and the bacon. Clean the swede, peel and cut into small pieces. Clean and/or peel the mirepoix vegetables and cut them into small pieces.

Heat the oil in a suitable pan and sauté the diced onion and bacon in it. Gradually stir in the prepared vegetables and cook for a few minutes, season with salt and pepper. Add the stock, bring to a boil and cook for about 20 minutes over medium heat. Then season to taste, ladle into 4 bowls, garnish with 1 tablespoon of sour cream and sprinkle with parsley.

Pea soup with ears and snouts

400 g peeled yellow peas, 1 bacon rind,
250 g cured pig ears, 250 g cured pig head (snout),
4 sprigs marjoram, 1 onion, 1 carrot, 1 parsley root,
1 leek, 250 g potatoes, salt, freshly ground pepper,
1 tbsp chopped parsley

Cover the peas with cold water and leave to soak for at least 8 hours. Then bring the soaking water to a boil with the bacon rind, pig ears and head, and the marjoram. Peel and mince the onion, carrot and parsley root. Cut the leek in half lengthwise, wash between the layers and slice crosswise into strips. Add the prepared vegetables and add more water if necessary. Simmer for about 2 hours on medium heat. Skim off any scum until the broth is clear.

Remove the pig ears and cut into thin strips. Remove the meat from the pig head and cut into small pieces. Peel and dice the potatoes. Put the meat back into the soup and leave to simmer for another 20 minutes. Lightly season with salt and pepper. Before serving, sprinkle with parsley. Serve with bread rolls.

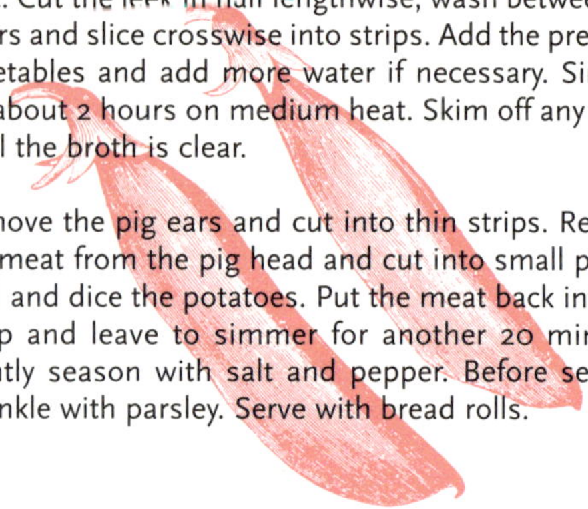

Aunt Gisela's lentil soup

1 onion, 100 g streaky bacon, small mirepoix of carrot with parsley root or celeriac and leek and parsley (or similar), 2 Teltow turnips, 2 tbsp vegetable oil, 250 g brown lentils, 1/8 l red wine, 2 bay leaves, 1 sprig thyme, 500 g cured pork chop on the bone, salt, freshly ground pepper, 50 g herbed crème fraîche

Peel and dice the onion. Dice the bacon. Clean and/or peel the mirepoix vegetables and cut into very small pieces. Peel and dice the turnips.

Heat the oil in a pan and sauté the diced onion and bacon in it. Add the prepared vegetables and cook for a few more minutes. Then add the lentils and cook for a few more minutes. Deglaze with the wine and add 2 litres of lukewarm water. Rinse the thyme and wash the pork chops. Add them with the bay leaves and cook the stew for 50 minutes over medium heat.

Take out the cured pork, remove the meat from the bone and cut into bite-size pieces. Season the soup with salt and pepper and stir in the crème fraîche. Portion the pieces of cured pork onto soup bowl plates and pour the hot soup over them.

Vegetable dishes – and plenty of potatoes

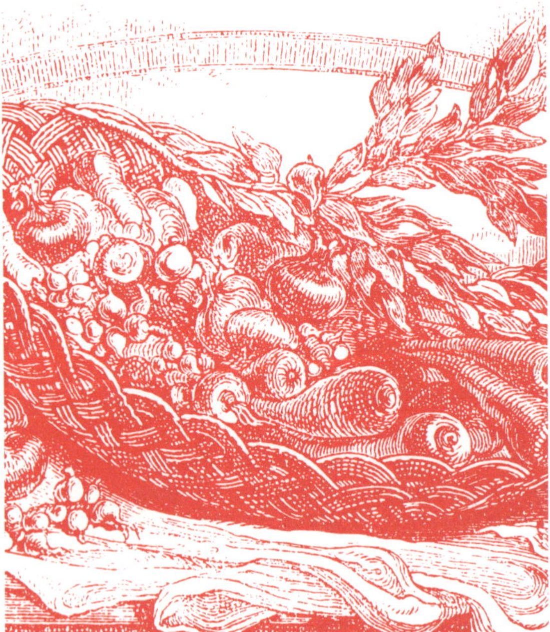

Mashed potatoes

1 kg floury potatoes, salt, 1 bay leaf, 1/4 l lukewarm milk, 2 tbsp butter at room temperature, 1 pinch freshly grated nutmeg

Peel the potatoes and cut them into pieces. Cook until done in lightly salted water with 1 bay leaf for about 30 minutes. Strain, and beat with a potato masher. Stir in the milk and butter and season with salt and nutmeg.

To make creamed potatoes, mash the potatoes and mix with around 3/8 litre milk and 2 tablespoons of butter and stir until smooth, season with salt, pepper and nutmeg.

Berlin-style potatoes boiled in meat stock

1/4 small mirepoix of carrot with parsley root or celeriac and leek and parsley (or similar), 800 g potatoes, 1 1/4 l meat stock, salt, freshly ground pepper, 1 pinch freshly grated nutmeg

Clean and/or peel all vegetables and dice them to 1 cm cubes. Cook in the stock for about 25 minutes on medium heat. Season with salt, pepper and nutmeg and portion the potatoes into heated bowls. Serve with boiled sausages, smoked pork chops or boiled meat.

Potato fritters

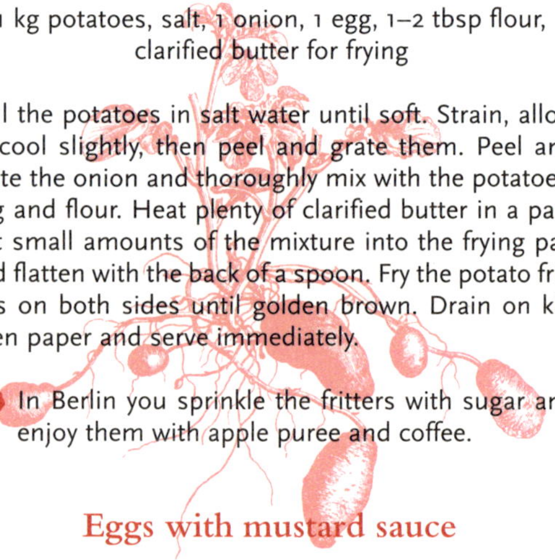

1 kg potatoes, salt, 1 onion, 1 egg, 1–2 tbsp flour, clarified butter for frying

Boil the potatoes in salt water until soft. Strain, allow to cool slightly, then peel and grate them. Peel and grate the onion and thoroughly mix with the potatoes, egg and flour. Heat plenty of clarified butter in a pan. Put small amounts of the mixture into the frying pan and flatten with the back of a spoon. Fry the potato fritters on both sides until golden brown. Drain on kitchen paper and serve immediately.

In Berlin you sprinkle the fritters with sugar and enjoy them with apple puree and coffee.

Eggs with mustard sauce

2 tbsp butter, 1 tbsp flour, 1 tbsp hot mustard, 1 tbsp sugar, 3 tbsp white wine vinegar, 1/4 l beef stock, salt, freshly ground black pepper, 8 soft-boiled eggs, 1 tbsp chopped parsley

Make a brown roux using the butter and flour. Stir in the mustard, sugar, vinegar and stock and cook to a creamy consistency. Add salt and pepper. Peel and halve the eggs. Portion 4 halves onto heated plates, cover with the sauce and sprinkle with the parsley.

Pea puree

A butcher's platter or smoked pork chops, knuckle of pork or eggs in mustard sauce (recipes p. 60, p. 62 and p. 34) without pea puree? Inconceivable!

400 g dried yellow peas, 100 g celeriac, 1 carrot, 1 parsley root, 1 bacon rind, 2 stems each marjoram and thyme, 1/4 bunch parsley, 1 onion, 100 g smoked streaky bacon, 1 tbsp clarified butter, salt, freshly ground pepper

Soak the peas in 400 millilitres of cold water for around 8 hours. Then bring to a boil in the soaking water. Clean and/or peel the vegetables and mince them. Add the rind and the washed herbs and allow to cook, covered, for 1 1/4 hours. Just before the end of the cooking period, peel the onion and mince it and the bacon, then sauté both in the clarified butter. Rinse the parsley, pat dry, pluck off and mince the leaves, then add them to the pan and sauté. Remove the herbs and bacon from the pan and set aside. Using a mixer, puree the peas well, season them with the salt and pepper, sprinkle with the onion, diced bacon and parsley, and serve.

„Leipziger Allerlei“ (mixed vegetables)

The *Allerlei* is a classic spring dish of traditional fine home cooking. It used to be much more lavishly prepared, and served on a platter with a whole cooked cauliflower in the middle. The other vegetables were cooked in a béchamel sauce and neatly arranged around the cauliflower together with crayfish.

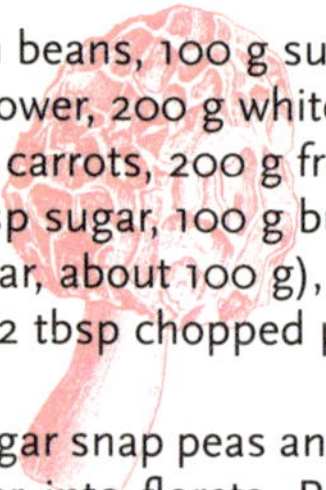

200 g fine green beans, 100 g sugar snap peas, 1 small cauliflower, 200 g white asparagus, 1 small kohlrabi, 2 carrots, 200 g fresh morel mushrooms, salt, 1 tbsp sugar, 100 g butter, shrimp or crayfish butter (jar, about 100 g), freshly ground pepper, 2 tbsp chopped parsley

Clean the beans, sugar snap peas and cauliflower. Separate the cauliflower into florets. Peel the asparagus and cut off the woody ends. Cut off the asparagus tips and put to one side. Cut the remaining asparagus spears into finger-width pieces. Peel the kohlrabi and carrots and cut into pencil-thick pieces. Thoroughly wash the morels.

Heat a large serving platter in the oven at 50 °C. In a large saucepan, bring to a boil plenty of water with 1 tablespoon of salt, sugar and 1 tablespoon of butter. Gently boil the beans, cauliflower, asparagus pieces, kohlrabi and carrots for 10 minutes. Remove the vegetables with a skimmer and drain through a large sieve. Leave the cooking water on the stove.

In the meantime, heat the prawn or crayfish butter in a large pan at very low heat. Toss the vegetables in it, season with pepper, arrange on the serving plate and keep warm in the oven preheated to 50 °C. Place the sugar snap peas and asparagus tips in the cooking water and boil for 5 minutes. Remove and drain. Toss in the prawn or crayfish butter, add pepper and add to the remaining vegetables in the oven.

Heat the remaining butter in a second pan, add the morels and fry at high heat for around 2 minutes, stirring constantly. Cover and cook for another 3 minutes on medium heat. Season with salt and pepper and pour over the vegetables.

Drizzle the *Allerlei* with the remaining prawn or crayfish butter, sprinkle with parsley and serve immediately. This goes well with potato dumplings.

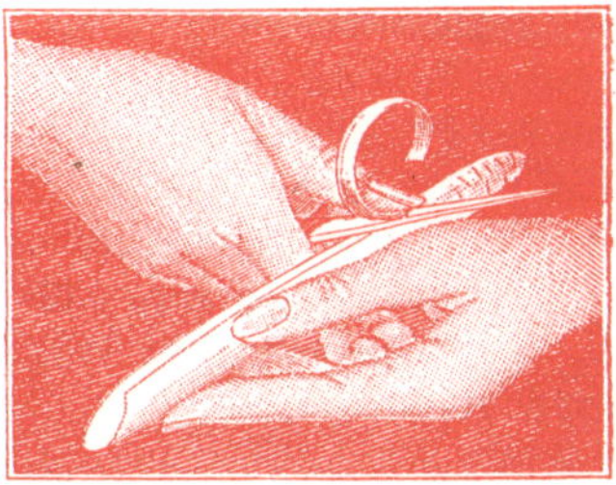

Teltow turnips

1 kg Teltow turnips, 4 tbsp butter, 2 tbsp sugar,
1/8 l beef or vegetable stock, salt, freshly ground pepper

Clean the turnips and cut into halves or quarters depending on their size. In a wide saucepan heat the butter and melt the sugar in it. Add the turnips and toss them in the caramel, deglaze with the stock and cook for 30 minutes. Season with salt and pepper.

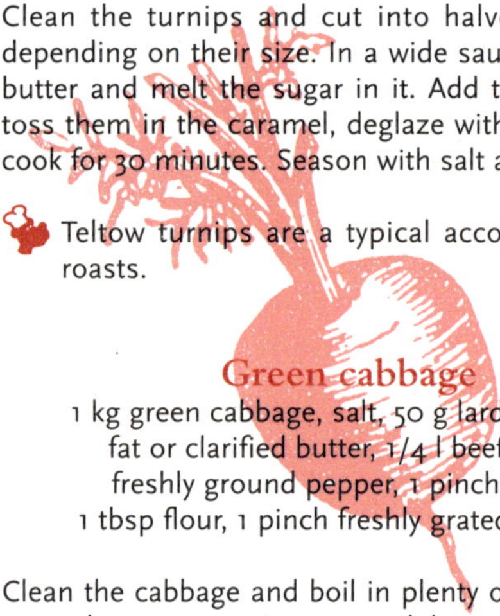

Teltow turnips are a typical accompaniment to roasts.

Green cabbage

1 kg green cabbage, salt, 50 g lard or goose
fat or clarified butter, 1/4 l beef stock,
freshly ground pepper, 1 pinch sugar,
1 tbsp flour, 1 pinch freshly grated nutmeg

Clean the cabbage and boil in plenty of salt water for around 10 minutes. Remove and drain through a sieve. Remove the leaves from the stem and chop them fine. Heat the fat in a wide saucepan and sauté the cabbage in it for around 10 minutes. Pour in the stock, season with the salt, pepper and sugar, cover and cook the cabbage for about 40 minutes. Dust with some flour and stir in well to thicken the sauce slightly. Season with salt, pepper and nutmeg.

For a more tangy flavour you can add some left-over ham.

In Berlin, people like eating the green cabbage with roast goose, duck or smoked pork chops.

Braised cucumbers

To the south of Berlin you find the Spreewald forest, which is world-famous for its cucumber specialities. It's no surprise then that they're also very popular in the capital itself.

800 g cucumbers (about 3), 1 onion, 50 g smoked streaky bacon, 2 tbsp vegetable oil, 1 pinch sugar, salt, freshly ground pepper, 1 splash white wine vinegar, 100 ml cream, 8 sprigs dill, minced

Peel the cucumbers and cut into half lengthwise, remove the seeds with a spoon and slice the cucumbers crosswise. Peel the onion and chop it and the bacon fine. Heat the oil in a wide saucepan and sauté the chopped onion and bacon in it. Add the cucumbers and stew the lot in its own juices for about 10 minutes while gently shaking the saucepan back and forth. Add water if necessary. Season the cucumbers with sugar, salt, pepper and vinegar and top the dish off with the cream. Stir in the dill just before serving.

Fish and meat dishes – from Havel pike perch to knuckle of pork

Havel pike-perch

Berlin does not just have rivers and lakes within its city borders, it is also surrounded by them. No wonder then that the cuisine of Berlin includes many fish dishes. This is one of the most famous ones, named after the Havel river to the west of Berlin.

4 pieces of pike perch (about 200 g each),
juice of 1 lemon, salt, freshly ground pepper,
50 g clarified butter, 2 tbsp flour for coating,
1 tbsp butter, 1 tbsp chopped dill

Rinse the slices of fish under cold running water and pat dry with kitchen towel. Drizzle with the lemon juice and season with salt and pepper; put aside and allow to marinate for a few minutes. Heat the clarified butter in a frying pan. Coat the pieces of fish with the flour and place in the pan. Cook the fish for about 10 minutes, slide the butter into the pan and turn the fish several times. Portion the pieces of pike perch onto 4 plates, drizzle with the juices from the pan and sprinkle with dill.

This is served with braised cucumbers (recipe p. 39) and boiled potatoes with butter.

Eel green from the Spreewald forest

Many traditional restaurants still serve this speciality dish in its original form: with new potatoes boiled in their skins and cucumber salad. The cucumbers have to be from the Spreewald forest, of course. You won't regret trying this dish at home.

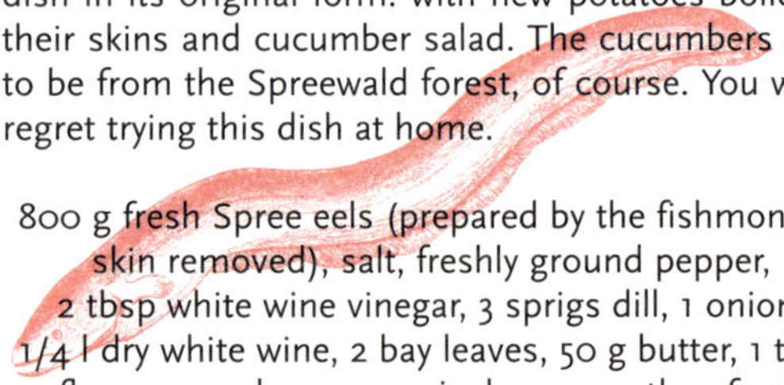

800 g fresh Spree eels (prepared by the fishmonger, skin removed), salt, freshly ground pepper, 2 tbsp white wine vinegar, 3 sprigs dill, 1 onion, 1/4 l dry white wine, 2 bay leaves, 50 g butter, 1 tbsp flour, 200 ml cream, 1 pinch sugar, 1 tbsp fresh lemon juice, 1 egg yolk, 4 tbsp freshly chopped dill for garnish

Rinse the eel, pat dry with kitchen towel, cut into 5-centimetre pieces and season with salt and pepper. Drizzle with vinegar and allow to marinate for a few minutes.

Meanwhile, rinse the dill and chop. Wash the unpeeled onion and chop it rough.

In a saucepan, bring 1/4 litre of water and the wine to a boil. Add the dill, chopped onion and bay leaves and reduce the heat. Add the pieces of eel to the slightly simmering broth and cook for about 15 minutes on medium heat or until tender. Take out the fish using a slotted spoon and put on a plate. Strain the broth through a fine sieve.

Make a light roux with the butter and flour, deglaze with the eel broth and stir until smooth. Finish off with cream and season with salt, pepper, sugar and lemon juice. Take some of the sauce from the pan, whisk together with the egg yolk and stir the mixture into the saucepan (NB: make sure the sauce does not boil again). Arrange the eel on a large serving platter, pour the sauce over it and sprinkle with the chopped dill.

To make eel Old Berlin-style, season the prepared pieces of eel with salt and pepper. In a frying pan, heat 50 grams of butter and add 100 grams of finely grated stale rye bread. Place the pieces of eel on top, top with the 2 bay leaves and sprinkle with about 8 black peppercorns. Cover the pan, cook the pieces of eel at low heat for just under 20 minutes, turning them two to three times and gradually adding 1/4 litre of Berliner Weiße beer. To serve, remove the pieces of eel from the pan and portion onto plates. Season the pan juices with salt, pepper and lemon juice and pour the sauce over the fish.

Carp Polish-style

This is a traditional holiday recipe, which many families serve at Christmas time. *Soßenlebkuchen* is a special type of gingerbread slightly less sweet than and about as dry as the typical English or North American varieties sold as gingerbread men.

1 fresh carp (prepared and cut into pieces by the fishmonger), juice of 1 lemon, salt, freshly ground pepper, small mirepoix of carrot and parsley root or celeriac with leek and parsley (or similar), 2 small onions, 50 g butter, 1 bay leaf, 4 cloves, 1/4 l dark beer, 1 grated *Soßenlebkuchen* (100 g)

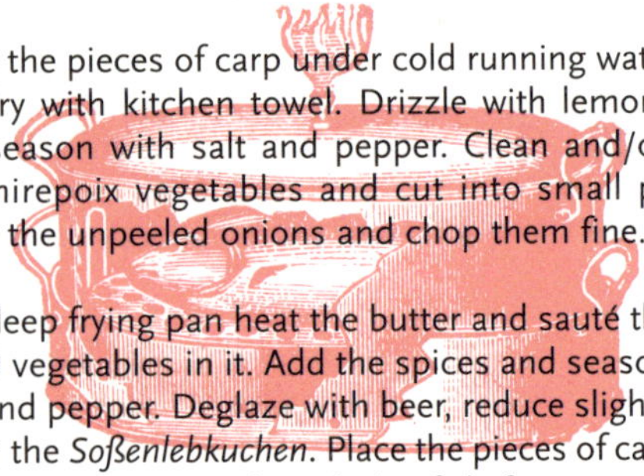

Rinse the pieces of carp under cold running water and pat dry with kitchen towel. Drizzle with lemon juice and season with salt and pepper. Clean and/or peel the mirepoix vegetables and cut into small pieces. Wash the unpeeled onions and chop them fine.

In a deep frying pan heat the butter and sauté the prepared vegetables in it. Add the spices and season with salt and pepper. Deglaze with beer, reduce slightly and stir in the *Soßenlebkuchen*. Place the pieces of carp into the sauce, cover, and cook the fish for 20 minutes, turning once or twice. Remove and portion onto plates. Strain the sauce through a fine sieve, season with salt and pepper and pour it over the fish.

Serve with boiled potatoes and a glass of beer.

Fried tench in dill butter

4 fresh tenches (about 350–400 g each, prepared by the fishmonger), juice of 1 lemon, salt, freshly ground pepper, 8 sprigs dill, 5–8 tbsp vegetable oil, 2 tbsp flour, 50 g butter, eighths of lemon for garnish

Rinse the tenches under cold running water, pat dry with kitchen towel, drizzle with lemon juice and season with salt and pepper.

Rinse the dill, pat dry and pluck off the leaves. Put about one third of it into the bellies of the fish and chop the rest fine.

Heat the oil in 2 large frying pans. Cover the fish with flour, shake off any excess, place into the pans and fry the tenches for 20 minutes, turning several times and adding butter. Remove from the pan and arrange on heated plates. Stir the dill quickly in the pan juices, drizzle the liquid over the fish and garnish with lemon eighths. Serve with boiled potatoes.

Perch in beer sauce

1 kg fresh perch (prepared by the fishmonger), juice of 1 lemon, salt, freshly ground pepper, 2 onions, 4 tbsp vegetable oil, 1 tsp brown sugar, 1 tsp flour, 1/4 l each light and dark beer, 3 cloves, 2 bay leaves, 1 tbsp white wine vinegar

Rinse the perch under cold running water, pat dry with kitchen towel, drizzle with lemon juice and season with salt and pepper. Peel and slice the onions fine. Heat the oil in a frying pan and sauté the onion in it until translucent. Sprinkle with sugar and flour and continue to sauté for a few minutes, stirring constantly. Gradually add the two types of beer with the cloves and bay leaves. Place the fish into the sauce, cover and cook for about 20 minutes. Remove from the pan and transfer to a heated serving platter. Strain the sauce through a fine sieve, season with salt, pepper and vinegar and pour over the fish. In Berlin you eat this dish with boiled potatoes.

Crayfish tails in dill sauce

Until the end of the 19th century basketfuls of the famous crayfish from the river Oder were sent from Berlin to Paris by overnight train. The waters around the capital used to teem with these wonderful crustaceans. Many of the recipes from that time can be found on menus in Berlin to this day, even though now the crayfish has to be imported. This is the Berliners' favourite crayfish tail recipe.

24 peeled crayfish tails, juice of 1/4 lemon,
salt, freshly ground pepper, 2 tbsp butter,
1 tsp flour, 1/4 l fish stock (jar), 200 ml cream,
1 egg yolk, a few splashes of Worcestershire sauce,
2 tbsp chopped dill

Rinse the crayfish tails, pat dry with kitchen towel, drizzle with lemon juice and season with salt and pepper. Heat the butter in a pan, stir in the flour and make a light roux. Whilst stirring add the stock and the cream, and keep stirring until smooth. Season with salt, pepper and Worcestershire sauce. Mix some of the sauce with the egg yolk and put the mix back into the pan. Place the crayfish tails into the pan, heat for 3–4 minutes and then stir in the dill.

Serve with rice – either as a ring of rice or pressed into cone-shaped moulds and turned out onto heated plates.

Chicken fricassee

There are many chicken fricassee recipes, from everyday to very posh (for example in the style of Hotel Adlon with tongue of veal, crayfish tails, black morels, sweetbread and asparagus). This is a simple recipe for the normal Berlin household and it always tastes great – or *knorke* as they say in Berlin.

1 fresh chicken (about 1 1/4 kg, prepared at the butcher shop), salt, mirepoix of carrot and parsley root or celeriac with leek and parsley (or similar), 2 tbsp butter, 1 tbsp flour, 200 ml cream, freshly ground white pepper, 1 egg yolk, 150 g (1 jar) button mushrooms, 300 g frozen peas, some lemon juice, 4 peeled crayfish tails, 100 g (1 jar) asparagus tips, 1 tbsp fresh chervil leaves

Rinse the chicken under cold running water inside and out. Place in a pan, cover with water and bring to a boil. As soon as the water boils, strain, add fresh cold water and bring to a boil again, then add the salt. Clean and/or peel the mirepoix vegetables, cut into small pieces and add to the pan. Cook the chicken over medium heat for about 1 1/4 hours or until done.

Remove the chicken, cut in half, and remove the skin and bones. Cut the meat into bite-size pieces. Strain the stock through a fine sieve. Heat the butter in a pan, stir in the flour and make a light roux, while gradually adding stock. Stir the sauce until creamy, add the cream and season with salt and pepper. Pour one ladle of sauce into a bowl, whisk the egg into it and stir it back into the pan (NB: make sure the sauce doesn't boil again).

Strain the mushrooms, stir into the sauce together with the peas and heat. Finally stir in the meat. Season with salt, pepper and some lemon juice. Place the chicken fricassee onto heated plates and garnish all around with asparagus tips. Place 1 crayfish tail in the middle of the dish. Finally rinse the chervil, pat it dry, and add as garnish.

Fresh (and cooked) button mushrooms and asparagus tips will of course make the dish a little more sophisticated.

Roast goose "Dönhoffplatz"

A well cooked goose is a gift from God, or, as they say in Berlin: *Ene jut jebratene Jans is ene jute Jabe Jottes.* And that's especially true at Christmas when roast goose is simply a must. People used to buy their geese on a Friday from the goose market at Dönhoffplatz, where you could buy your Sunday goose together with down for your feather duvet.

1 fresh goose (about 4 kg, prepared at
the butcher shop), salt, freshly ground pepper,
4 sprigs mugwort, 5 sour apples (such as russet),
2 onions, 1 tbsp cornflour

Preheat the oven to 180 °C (fan oven 160 °C, gas mark 4). Thoroughly rinse the goose under cold running water inside and out, removing the fat from inside the goose at the same time. Pat dry with kitchen towel, and season with salt and pepper inside and out.

Wash the mugwort and pat it dry. Cut the unpeeled apples into quarters and remove the cores. Stuff the goose with the apples and mugwort. Close the openings with kitchen twine and secure the legs to the body.

Put the goose into a roasting tin breast side up and pour about 200 millilitres of water into the pan. Place in the bottom of the oven and roast the goose for about 2 1/4 hours. About half-way through, pierce the goose just below the legs to allow the fat to drain from the meat. Peel and slice the onions, and arrange around the goose. Add around 1/4 litre of cold water.

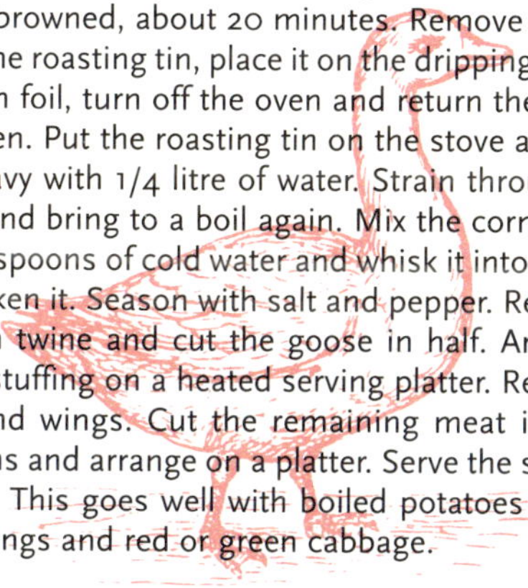

At the end of the cooking time, increase the temperature to 200 °C and turn on the grill until the goose is nicely browned, about 20 minutes. Remove the goose from the roasting tin, place it on the dripping pan lined with tin foil, turn off the oven and return the goose to the oven. Put the roasting tin on the stove and loosen the gravy with 1/4 litre of water. Strain through a fine sieve and bring to a boil again. Mix the cornflour with 3 tablespoons of cold water and whisk it into the sauce to thicken it. Season with salt and pepper. Remove the kitchen twine and cut the goose in half. Arrange the apple stuffing on a heated serving platter. Remove the legs and wings. Cut the remaining meat into small portions and arrange on a platter. Serve the sauce separately. This goes well with boiled potatoes or potato dumplings and red or green cabbage.

Mother Schulze's beef roulades

The true home of *Molle* (beer) is the pub, the local round the corner. And that's where you will often find a sign in the window saying *Futtern wie bei Muttern* (eat like you do at mother's). This may put some people off (depending on their mother's culinary skills), but Mother Schulze, who this recipe is named after, was an excellent cook.

4 slices of beef roulade (topside, about 180 g each),
salt, freshly ground pepper, 1 tbsp hot mustard,
4 thin rashers of smoked streaky bacon,
1 large onion, 1 large pickled gherkin,
small mirepoix of carrot and parsley root or celeriac
with leek and parsley (or similar), 1 tomato,
4 tbsp vegetable oil, 1/8 l red wine, 1/4 l beef stock,
2 tbsp of the gherkin pickling fluid,
2 bay leaves, a few black peppercorns,
200 ml cream, 4 toothpicks

Rinse the meat, pat dry and season with salt and pepper on both sides. Place on the worktop, coat with the mustard and place 1 rasher of bacon on each one. Peel and halve the onion and cut into very fine strips. Cut the gherkin into lengthwise strips. Put half of the onion and gherkin slices on top of the slices of meat, roll them up and secure them with toothpicks. Clean and/or peel the mirepoix vegetables and cut into large pieces. Core the tomato and cut it into quarters.

Heat the oil in a wide pan and sear the roulades on all sides. Place the remaining vegetables and tomato quarters around the meat and also fry. Pour in the wine, stock, and gherkin pickling fluid. Add bay leaves and peppercorns, cover and cook the roulades on medium heat for about 1 1/4 hours, turning several times and adding more water if necessary.

Remove the roulades, put on a plate, cover with tinfoil and leave to rest. Pass the sauce through a sieve, bring to a boil again, add the cream and season with salt and pepper. Mix the gravy from the pan into the sauce. Put the roulades onto heated plates and cover with the sauce. This goes well with mashed potatoes, red cabbage or mixed vegetables.

Stuffed cabbage

8 large white or savoy cabbage leaves, salt,
1 bread roll (from the previous day), 1 cup hot milk,
1 onion, 1 garlic clove, 50 g cooked ham,
2 tbsp butter, 500 g minced meat (half beef,
half pork), 1 egg, salt, freshly ground pepper,
grated peel of 1/4 unwaxed lemon, 1 tsp dried thyme,
1 tbsp freshly chopped herbs (e.g. parsley, chervil),
small mirepoix of carrot and parsley root or celeriac
with leek and parsley (or similar), 4 tbsp vegetable
oil, 1/4 l hot beef stock, 100 g crème fraîche

Wash the cabbage leaves and blanch them in boiling salt water for 1 minute. Drain, plunge into cold water and drain. Soak the bread roll in the hot milk. Peel the onion and garlic and dice them fine along with the bacon. Heat 1 teaspoon of butter in a pan and sauté the onion, garlic and bacon until the onion is translucent, allow to cool slightly. Place the contents of the pan in a bowl together with the egg, the squeezed-out bread roll and the mince, and knead into a smooth mass. Season with the salt, pepper, lemon peel and herbs.

Place the cabbage leaves on the worktop and cut off the tough outer ribs of the cabbage. Place some of the meat dough in the middle of each leaf, fold in the sides, roll into roulades and tie with kitchen twine.

Preheat the oven to 200 °C (fan oven 180 °C, gas mark 5). Clean and/or peel and chop the mirepoix vegetables fine.

Heat the oil and remaining butter in a heavy oven-proof pan with a lid, and brown the roulades on all sides. Add the mirepoix and sauté. Pour in the stock, briefly bring to a boil and cover the pan. Place in the middle of the oven and stew the roulades for about 1 1/4 hours. Remove and arrange on a heated serving platter. Pass the sauce through a fine sieve, bring to a boil again and stir in the crème fraîche. Season with salt and pepper before serving.

People used to thicken this sauce with cornflour, but in this recipe I have replaced it with the more contemporary crème fraîche.

Königsberg meatballs

Berliners simply love meatballs even though Berlin is not where they come from. The meatballs in this recipe are named after the capital of East Prussia, where they originate.

1 bread roll (from the previous day), 5 anchovy fillets, 1 small onion, 500 g minced meat (half beef, half pork), 1 egg, freshly ground pepper, 1 pinch freshly grated nutmeg, salt, 2 bay leaves, 2 tbsp butter, 1 tbsp flour, 150 ml dry white wine, 2 tbsp pickled capers, 1 tsp fresh lemon juice, 100 ml cream, 1 egg yolk, 1 pinch dried marjoram

Put the bread roll in a bowl and cover with lukewarm water. Rinse the anchovy fillets under cold running water, pat dry with kitchen towel and chop them fine. Peel the onion and dice it fine. Knead the mince, the squeezed-out bread roll, anchovies, diced onion and egg into a smooth mass. Season with pepper and nutmeg and leave to rest for a short while. Shape into walnut-size balls.

Heat salted water in a pan to boiling point. Add the bay leaves and the meatballs and cook for about 20 minutes until done. Remove and keep warm. Take 1/4 litre of the stock and put to one side.

Heat the butter in a pan and make a light roux with the flour. Deglaze with the wine, pour in the meatball stock that was set aside and stir well. Add the meatballs and capers to the pan. Stir in the cream and season the sauce with salt, pepper, and lemon juice. Just before serving, pour one ladle of soup into a bowl, whisk the egg into it and stir it back into the pan (NB: make sure the sauce does not boil again). Stir in the marjoram. Serve with boiled or mashed potatoes (recipe p. 33).

Liver with apple and onion

4 slices (about 150 g each) of pork or calf liver, freshly ground pepper, 2 tbsp flour, 2 large onions, 2 apples (e.g. russet), 2 tbsp vegetable oil, 3 tbsp butter, 8 thin rashers of streaky bacon, salt

Rinse the liver and pat it dry with paper towels, season with pepper, roll in flour, shaking off any excess. Peel the onions and slice into very thin rings. Peel the apples, remove the core with an apple corer and cut into slices.

In a frying pan, heat 1 tablespoon each of the oil and butter and sauté the onions until translucent. At the same time, fry the bacon in another pan until crisp without adding any fat. Remove the bacon and leave to drain on kitchen roll. Add 1 tablespoon of butter to the remaining fat and heat. Fry the slices of liver for 5 minutes on each side, remove and keep warm. Remove the onion rings from the pan, add the remaining butter and fry the apple slices in the butter on both sides. Lightly season the liver with salt and arrange on heated plates. Top with onion rings and 2 rashers of bacon each and place the apple slices on top. Be sure to serve with mashed potatoes (recipe p. 33) and beer, and perhaps a green salad.

Schnitzel à la Holstein

During the time of Emperor Wilhelm II, Privy Councillor Holstein II became a part of culinary history when he visited the legendary restaurant, Borchardt, and asked to be served a dish prepared according to his own instructions: the schnitzel that was later to carry his name.

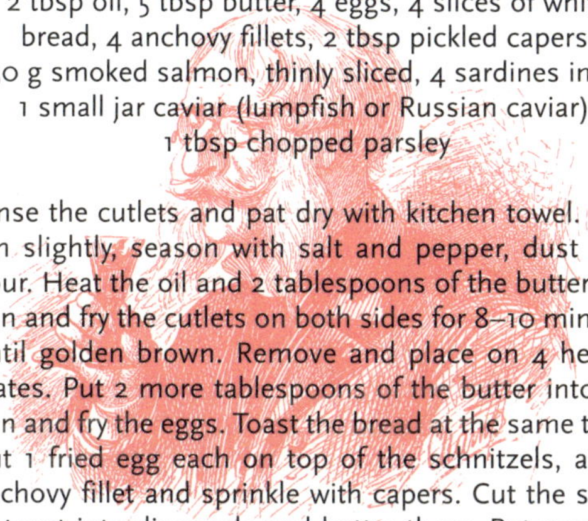

4 veal cutlets (about 150 g each), salt,
freshly ground pepper, flour to dust the meat,
2 tbsp oil, 5 tbsp butter, 4 eggs, 4 slices of white
bread, 4 anchovy fillets, 2 tbsp pickled capers,
150 g smoked salmon, thinly sliced, 4 sardines in oil,
1 small jar caviar (lumpfish or Russian caviar),
1 tbsp chopped parsley

Rinse the cutlets and pat dry with kitchen towel. Flatten slightly, season with salt and pepper, dust with flour. Heat the oil and 2 tablespoons of the butter in a pan and fry the cutlets on both sides for 8–10 minutes until golden brown. Remove and place on 4 heated plates. Put 2 more tablespoons of the butter into the pan and fry the eggs. Toast the bread at the same time. Put 1 fried egg each on top of the schnitzels, add 1 anchovy fillet and sprinkle with capers. Cut the slices of toast into diagonals and butter them. Put some of the salmon and 1 sardine on each half. Sprinkle with caviar and parsley. Serve the schnitzel with 2 halves of toast each. This goes well with fried potatoes and buttered green beans.

Kasseler cured pork chops with sauerkraut

Around 100 years ago, master butcher Johann Cassel from Potsdamer Straße had the clever idea of immersing pork chops in ten percent brine solution before smoking them – for 5 whole days. And that's where the Kasseler originates – in Berlin and not in the town of Kassel, as one might surmise. Back then, the salted and smoked pieces of Kasseler were fried in plenty of clarified butter on both sides and served with fried potatoes. Only later did this dish become a roast – either with a nice brown crust or wrapped in delicate puff pastry, and served with red cabbage or sauerkraut and mashed potatoes (recipe p. 33).

1 kg Kasseler, 5 onions, 2 cloves, 4 bay leaves,
1 carrot, 1 apple, 2 tbsp lard,
750 g sauerkraut, 100 ml dry white wine,
1 tbsp black peppercorns, salt, 100 ml cream

Preheat the oven to 200 °C (fan oven 180 °C, gas mark 5). Put the piece of Kasseler into a roasting tin with the fatty side up. Peel 1 onion, stud with cloves and 2 bay leaves and add it to the meat in the tin. Peel and slice the carrot and sprinkle it over the rest. Pour in 1/4 litre of boiling water. Place the roasting tin in the lower half of the oven and cook for 30 minutes, turning 2 to 3 times and adding water if necessary.

In the meantime, peel the remaining onions and cut into wafer-thin slices. Heat the lard in a pan and sauté the onion in it. Peel and core the apple, cut into thin slices and stir in. Using a fork, tease apart the sauerkraut and add it to the pan. Pour in the wine and some Kasseler gravy from the roasting tin, add peppercorns and the remaining bay leaves and cook the sauerkraut for about 20 minutes, then season with salt.

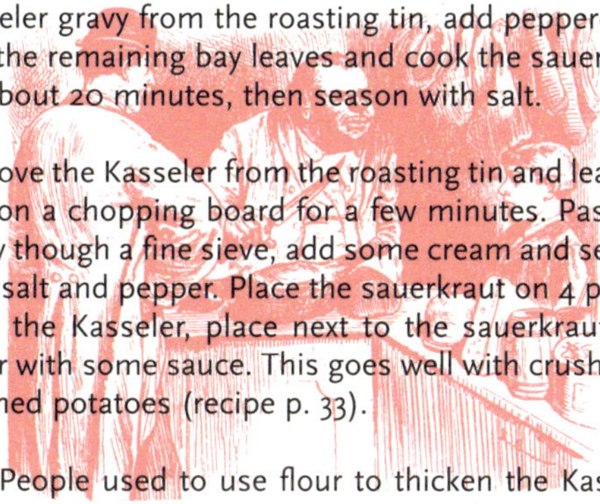

Remove the Kasseler from the roasting tin and leave to rest on a chopping board for a few minutes. Pass the gravy though a fine sieve, add some cream and season with salt and pepper. Place the sauerkraut on 4 plates. Slice the Kasseler, place next to the sauerkraut and cover with some sauce. This goes well with crushed or mashed potatoes (recipe p. 33).

People used to use flour to thicken the Kasseler gravy, today you use cream instead.

In Berlin, people eat the leftover Kasseler cold the next day with mustard or Cumberland sauce, and serve it with potato salad (recipe p. 16).

Knuckle of pork with broth

1 1/4 kg salted knuckle of pork (pre-ordered from the butcher and divided into 4 portions), 2 onions, mirepoix of carrot and parsley root or celeriac with leek and parsley (or similar), 2 cloves, 2 bay leaves, 1 tsp black and white peppercorns

Thoroughly rinse the knuckle of pork under cold running water to remove any fragments of bone. Cover with cold water in a large pan and bring to a boil. Skim the stock until it is clear.

In the meantime, peel and chop the onions. Clean and/or peel and chop the mirepoix vegetables. Add the prepared vegetables, cloves, bay leaves and peppercorns to the pan. Cook the knuckle of pork at medium heat with the lid on for about 1 1/4 hours until done. Remove and portion into 4 bowls. Drizzle with stock and serve.

This is of course served with pea puree (recipe p. 35) and sauerkraut (recipe p. 60) – usually with a glass of beer and a shot of Korn schnapps.

"Hoppel-Poppel"

This is a very delicious dish made from leftovers. It'll be just as tasty, of course, if you use fresh ingredients.

1 large onion, 250 g leftovers from roast or
other cooked meat, 4 tbsp butter,
500 g potatoes boiled in their skin and sliced,
salt, freshly ground pepper, 2 eggs

Peel and halve the onion, slice one half and mince the other. Cut the leftover meat into fine slices.

Heat 2 tablespoons of the butter in each of 2 frying pans. Put the minced onion and sliced meat in one, and the onion slices and potatoes in the other, season everything with salt and pepper, and sauté. As soon as the potatoes are nicely browned, put them in the first pan and gently fold them in, making sure that the potatoes don't get mushy. Whisk the eggs, pour into the pan, stir until creamy and serve the dish immediately from the pan.

There is also a drink called Hoppel-Poppel, which is very popular in Berlin. To make the drink, beat until creamy 4 egg yolks with 3 tablespoons of sugar and 200 millilitres of cream in a heatproof bowl over a bain-marie. The mixture is poured into punch glasses, dusted with freshly grated nutmeg and served immediately.

"Falscher Hase" meatloaf

Many regional cuisines have their own meatloaf version. In Berlin, this dish is made by wrapping the meat mixture around hard-boiled eggs and shaping everything into a pretty loaf.

2 bread rolls (from previous day),
100 g smoked streaky bacon, 2 onions,
1 tsp butter, 1 kg minced meat (half pork, half beef),
2 eggs, 1/4 tsp dried marjoram, salt,
freshly ground pepper, 1 generous pinch each hot
and sweet paprika powder, 1 tsp hot mustard,
1 tbsp clarified butter, 1/4 l hot beef stock,
250 g baby carrots, 200 ml cream,
1 tbsp freshly chopped parsley

Cut the bread rolls into small pieces and cover with about 200 millilitres of cold water. Mince the bacon. Peel and mince the onions.

Place the minced meat in a bowl. In a pan, render the diced bacon and add to the mince. Heat some butter in the pan and sauté the diced onion in it until translucent. Also add to the mince.

Knead all the ingredients together with the squeezed-out bread roll pieces and the eggs into a smooth mass. Season with marjoram, salt, pepper, paprika and mustard. Shape the mixture into an oval loaf.

Preheat the oven to 200 °C (fan oven 180 °C, gas mark 3). Heat the clarified butter in a roasting tin, put the meatloaf in it and sear on all sides. Put the roasting tin in the middle of the oven and cook the meatloaf for 50 minutes, pouring hot beef stock over it several times. Just before the end of the cooking time put the cleaned baby carrots all around the *Falscher Hase*.

Remove the roasting tin from the oven, carefully remove the meat and the carrots and put to one side. Briefly bring the roasting juices to a boil, pass through a fine sieve, bring to a boil again, season with salt and pepper and add cream. Cut the meatloaf into thick slices and place on heated plates together with the carrots. Drizzle with the sauce and sprinkle with parsley.

This dish goes well with red cabbage and mashed or crushed potatoes (recipe p. 33) or swede.

"Stolzer Heinrich"

This is a rich bratwurst dish. The menus of traditional restaurants list it under the name of "Stolzer Heinrich" ("proud Henry") or as "Bratwurst in beer sauce".

4 bratwurst sausages from Berlin (not boiled, about 150 g each), 100 g smoked streaky bacon, 1 onion, 4 tbsp butter, 1/4 l light or dark beer, 2 bay leaves, 5 black peppercorns, 1 tbsp cornflour, salt, freshly ground pepper

Using a sharp fork pierce the bratwurst sausages several times all over and pour boiling water over them. Drain on kitchen towel and pat dry. Mince the bacon, peel and slice the onion. Fry the bacon in a pan without adding fat, remove and place on a plate.

Heat the butter in a pan and sauté the onions until translucent. Add the sausages and sear on all sides. Pour in the beer, add the bay leaves and peppercorns and thicken the sauce for 10 minutes on medium heat. Remove sausages from the pan and put onto 4 plates. Allow the onion and beer sauce to reduce further and thicken it with the dissolved cornflour. Remove the bay leaves, season the sauce with salt and pepper and pour over the bratwurst sausages. This goes well with mashed potatoes (recipe p. 33).

Egg noodles with "Beamtenstippe"

This is a single forlorn noodle recipe amongst the many potato dishes from Berlin.

3 tbsp vegetable oil, 250 g minced seasoned pork with onion (prepared by the butcher), 1 tbsp tomato puree, salt, freshly ground pepper, 1 tsp marjoram, 1/4 l chicken stock, 500 g egg noodles of your choice

Heat the oil in a pan, and fry the mince until crumbly, add the tomato puree and brown lightly. Season with salt, pepper and marjoram and add the stock. Cook the *Beamtenstippe* over low heat for another 10 minutes, stirring occasionally.

In the meantime, cook the noodles al dente in plenty of boiling salted water for about 10 minutes. Drain, ladle into bowls and serve with the *Beamtenstippe* sauce.

Desserts and pastries – from "Rote Grütze" to pancakes

"Berliner Luft" ("Berlin air" or mousse) with red fruit

4 eggs, 200 g sugar, 1 tbsp cornflour,
100 ml apple juice, juice of 1 lemon, 200 ml cream,
1 sachet vanilla sugar, 500 g mixed berries
(strawberries, raspberries, black currants)

Mix the eggs, 150 grams of sugar, cornflour and apple and lemon juice in a heatproof bowl and beat to a creamy consistency over a bain-marie. Remove the bowl from the pan and beat the mixture over a cold bain-marie until cold. Whip the cream with the vanilla sugar until stiff and fold into the creamy mixture. Cover the bowl with cling film and put in the fridge for around 2 hours.

In the meantime, wash the berries and cut the strawberries into small pieces. Bring 150 millilitres of water to a boil together with the remaining sugar. Add the berries and let simmer for a few minutes. Remove from the heat and leave to cool a little. Put the mousse into dishes and serve the lukewarm berries separately.

"Rote Grütze" with fruit from the Werder region

In the south, just outside Berlin, you find the Werder region – a true fruit and vegetable haven. Every year they celebrate the Werder (cherry) tree blossom festival, offering a great choice of everything from sweet and sour cherries and many types of berry, through to apples, pears and plums. Berliners like to celebrate their own private tree blossom festival with *Rote Grütze* (red fruit jelly) served with a good dollop of cream.

800 g fresh red berries (raspberries, red currants) and pitted (sweet and sour) cherries, 150 g sugar, 3 tbsp cornflour, 200 ml cream

Clean the fruit if necessary and place in a wide pan. Bring to a boil with 250 millilitres of water and 120 grams of the sugar, then reduce the heat. Mix the cornflour with a little of the fruit liquid and add to the pan to thicken the mixture. Pour into a serving bowl. Sprinkle the remaining sugar over the jelly and leave to cool. Serve with the cream.

Puff pastry "Schuhsohlen"

Berliners have a sweet tooth, and they love a piece of pastry like this one served with their chicory coffee or latte – always with plenty of whipped cream.

200 g sheets of puff pastry (frozen),
50 g coarse sugar, 400 ml cream, 2 sachets vanilla sugar, caster sugar or icing sugar for garnish

Defrost the sheets of puff pastry by placing them next to each other on the worktop. Preheat the oven to 200 °C (fan oven 180 °C, gas mark 5). Cut out 7 centimetre circles of pastry dough. Sprinkle the worktop with some coarse sugar, place the pastry circles onto the sugar and roll into oval shapes ("shoe soles"). Place on a baking tray lined with greaseproof paper. Bake in the middle of the oven for just under 10 minutes or until they are a crisp golden brown. Remove to a rack and leave to cool. Whip the cream with vanilla sugar until stiff and put into a piping bag with a star-shaped nozzle. Pipe cream over half the *Schuhsohlen*. Place the remaining puff pastry soles on top and sprinkle with caster sugar or dust with icing sugar.

Doughnuts/Kameruners

These are called *Pfannkuchen* in Berlin – which means 'pancakes' in the rest of Germany. These filled pastries are made from a fluffy yeast dough and taste particularly good when homemade. In the city's west they are round, but in the east they have a twisted shape and are called Kameruners. So why not make some of both delicious treats from Berlin, using the dough described below.

For the dough: 500 g flour, 42 g fresh yeast, 50 g sugar, 1/4 l lukewarm milk, 100 g butter (room temperature), a pinch of salt, grated peel of 1/4 unwaxed lemon, 3 egg yolks
For the filling: jam (apricot, cherry, raspberry or plum etc.)
Plus: flour for dusting, 1 kg fat for deep-frying, icing sugar for dusting or sugar for coating

To make the dough, sieve the flour into a bowl and make a well in the middle. Crumble the yeast into it, sprinkle with sugar and pour in the milk. Dust with a bit of flour and scatter flakes of butter all over it. Cover the bowl and allow the mixture to rise in a warm, draught-free place for about 30 minutes. Add the salt, lemon peel and egg yolks and knead into a smooth dough. Cover and leave to rise for another hour.

To make doughnuts, knead the dough well on a floured worktop and roll out to 3 millimetres. On half the dough mark (don't cut) circles using a glass or a cup. Place 1 teaspoon of jam in the middle of each circle and place the second sheet of dough on top. Cut out the filled dough circles with a cup or a glass and press the edges together firmly.

Turn the doughnuts over onto a floured worktop, cover with a cloth and leave to rise for another 30 minutes by which time they should have visibly risen.

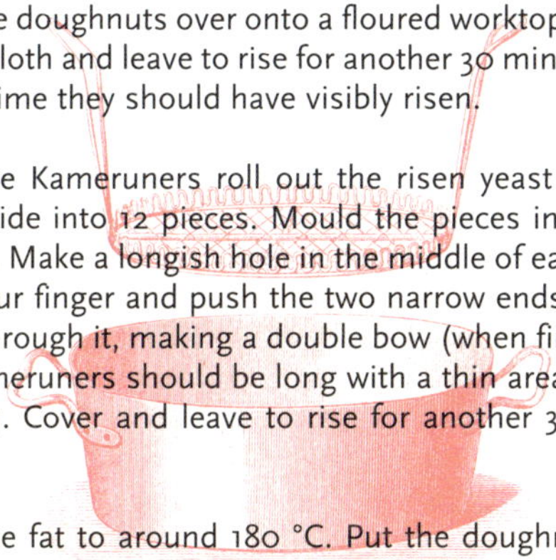

To make Kameruners roll out the risen yeast dough and divide into 12 pieces. Mould the pieces into oval shapes. Make a longish hole in the middle of each one with your finger and push the two narrow ends of the ovals through it, making a double bow (when finished, the Kameruners should be long with a thin area in the middle). Cover and leave to rise for another 30 minutes.

Heat the fat to around 180 °C. Put the doughnuts or Kameruners into the fat one by one and fry the floating pastry pieces to a crisp golden brown. Remove from the fat and drain on a cake rack. Dust the doughnuts immediately with the icing sugar and coat the Kameruners with sugar or cover with icing. Enjoy them as soon as possible.

"Liebesknochen" (éclairs)

This recipe reflects the influence of the Huguenots on Berlin's cuisine. The Berliners simply renamed their éclairs and called them *Liebesknochen* ("love bones").

For the choux pastry: 150 ml milk, 1 tbsp sugar,
pinch of salt, 100 g butter, 150 g flour, 4 eggs
For the filling: 1/4 l milk, 1 sachet vanilla sugar,
3 egg yolks, 100 g sugar, 1 tbsp flour,
2 tbsp instant coffee powder, 2 egg whites
Plus: 200 g icing sugar, 2 tbsp cocoa,
1 tbsp melted butter

To make the choux pastry, put the milk, 150 millilitres of water, sugar, salt and butter into a pan and bring to a boil. Remove the pan from the heat and stir in the flour all at once. Put the pan back on the heat and beat the mixture with a wooden spoon until the dough comes away from the bottom of the pan in a single lump. Remove the pan from the heat again and stir in the eggs one by one. Preheat the oven to 200 °C (fan oven 180 °C, gas mark 5) and cover a baking tray with greaseproof paper. Put portions of the dough into a piping bag with a star-shaped nozzle and pipe out 12 strips of around 10 centimetres about 4 cm apart. Place the baking tray in the middle of the oven and bake the dough strips for about 30 minutes or until golden brown. Remove from the tray and leave to cool on a wire rack.

In the meantime, put the milk and vanilla sugar in a pan and bring to a boil. Remove from the heat. Using an electric hand mixer, mix the egg yolk and sugar in a heatproof bowl over a bain-marie until creamy. Stir in the flour and cocoa. Gradually mix in the milk until you have a thick creamy mixture. Beat the egg white until stiff and fold in. Leave the mousse to cool a little.

Make a lengthwise slit in the side of each of the strips of dough, but do not cut right through. Put the mousse into a piping bag and pipe into the openings.

To make the icing, warm the icing sugar, cocoa and butter in a pan, stir until creamy and brush it on the surface of the *Liebesknochen*. Keep the éclairs in a cool place until the icing has set and then serve as soon as possible.

"Streuselkuchen" (crumble cake)

For the dough: 500 g flour, 20 g fresh yeast, 50 g sugar, 1/4 l lukewarm milk, 80 g butter (room temperature), pinch of salt
For the crumble: 200 g flour, 200 g sugar, 1/4 tsp ground cinnamon, 150 g cold butter
Plus: flour for dusting, 200 ml cream

To make the dough, sieve the flour into a bowl and make a well in the middle. Crumble the yeast into it, sprinkle with sugar and pour in the milk. Dust with a bit of the flour. Cover the bowl and allow the mixture to rise in a warm, draught-free place for about 30 minutes. Add the salt, knead the mixture into a smooth dough, cover with a cloth and leave to rise for another 30 minutes.

Briefly knead the dough on a floured worktop and roll out to the size of a baking tray. Place the dough on a baking tray lined with greaseproof paper. Pull up the edges of the paper and once again leave to rise for 30 minutes.

Preheat the oven to 200 °C (fan oven 180 °C, gas mark 5). For the crumble, dice the butter. Quickly hack into the mixed flour, sugar, and cinnamon with two knives until crumbly. Distribute the crumble evenly all over the rolled-out dough.

Put the baking tray into the middle of the oven and bake the crumble cake for about 30 minutes until golden yellow. Remove, leave to cool for a short while and cut into individual portions. Serve with whipped cream.

To make a special Sunday cake, add 50 grams of chopped almonds to the crumble.

Bee sting cake

For the dough: 500 g flour, 42 g fresh yeast, 100 g sugar, 1/4 l lukewarm milk, 100 g butter at room temperature, 2 eggs, pinch of salt
For the topping: 150 g butter, 180 g sugar, 1 sachet vanilla sugar, 150 g flaked almonds, 5 tbsp milk
For the filling: 1/4 l milk, 1 sachet custard powder, pinch of salt, 50 g sugar, 150 g melted butter
Plus: flour for dusting

To make the dough, sieve the flour into a bowl and make a well in the middle. Crumble the yeast into it, sprinkle with sugar, pour the milk in and dust with a bit of flour from the edge. Cover the bowl and allow the mixture to rise in a warm, draught-free place for about 20 minutes. Then knead into a smooth dough with the butter, eggs and salt, cover and leave to rise for another 20 minutes.

Preheat the oven to 200 °C (fan oven 180 °C, gas mark 5) and line a baking tray with greaseproof paper. Briefly knead the dough again on the worktop, roll out to the size of the baking tray, about one finger thick. Place on the baking tray and prick all over with a fork. Leave to rise for another 10 minutes.

In the meantime, heat the butter, sugar and vanilla sugar for the topping in a pan, stirring constantly. Gently stir in the almond flakes and then the milk. Remove the pan from the heat and leave the mixture to cool

until spreadable. Then spread the mixture evenly over the rolled-out dough. Place the baking tray in the middle of the oven and bake the cake for about 30 minutes or until golden brown. Remove from the oven and leave to cool.

To make the filling, mix the custard powder and 5 tablespoons of the milk until smooth. Put the remaining milk and sugar in a pan with the salt and bring to a boil. Stir in the custard powder and milk mixture. Bring to a boil and remove from the heat.

Whisk the butter into the custard. Cut the cake into 4 pieces of equal size and cut each piece in half horizontally. Spread the bottom halves with the creamy custard and replace the tops. Before serving, leave the cake in a cool place for about 2 hours and then cut into individual portions.

Index

Snacks – from meatballs to curried sausage

Soups and stews – not just with lentils and peas

Vegetable dishes – and plenty of potatoes

Fish and meat dishes – from Havel pike perch to knuckle of pork

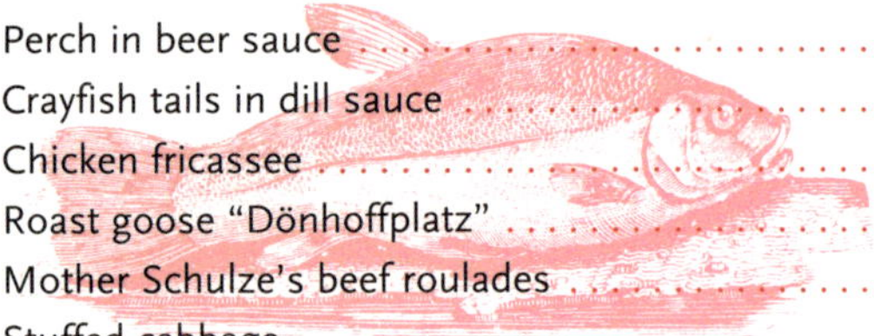

Desserts and pastries – from "Rote Grütze" to pancakes